THE Divas' COLLECTION

CONTENTS

Project Manager: CAROL CUELLAR
Art Design: CARMEN FORTUNATO

ALWAYS BE MY BABY

Words and Music by
MANUEL SEAL, JERMAINE DUPRI
and MARIAH CAREY

4

Now you want to be free,_____ so I'll let you fly._____
But in - ev - i - ta - bly,_____ you'll be back a - gain._____

'Cause I know in my heart,__ babe,_____ our____ love____ will nev - er die,__ no. }
'Cause you know in your heart,__ babe,_____ our____ love____ will nev - er end,__ no. }

Chorus:

You'll al - ways be a part of me,___ I'm part of you in - def - i - nite - ly._____

6

Chorus:

ANYONE AT ALL

Words and Music by
CAROLE KING
and CAROLE BAYER SAGER

Moderately slow ♩ = 92

1. Fun-ny how_ I feel more my-self with you than an-y-bod-y else that I ev-er knew._ I hear it in_ your voice, see it in_ your face. You've be-come the

2. Was-n't in_ the plan, not that I could see. Sud-den-ly_ a mir-a-cle came_ to me._ Safe with-in_ your arms, I can say_ what's true. Noth-ing in the

Anyone At All - 5 - 1

10

BECAUSE YOU LOVED ME
(Theme from "Up Close & Personal")

Words and Music by
DIANE WARREN

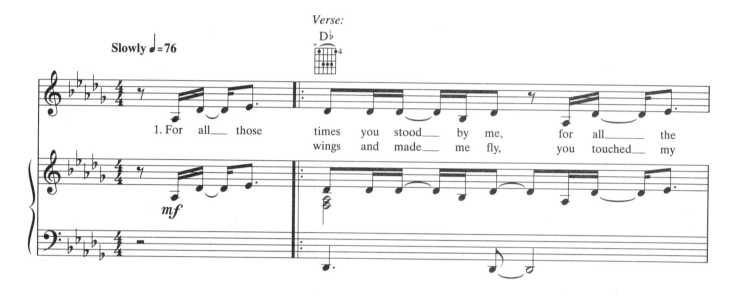

Because You Loved Me - 5 - 1

Because You Loved Me - 5 - 2

FALLING INTO YOU

Words and Music by
MARIE CLAIRE D'UBALDO,
BILLY STEINBERG and RICK NOWLES

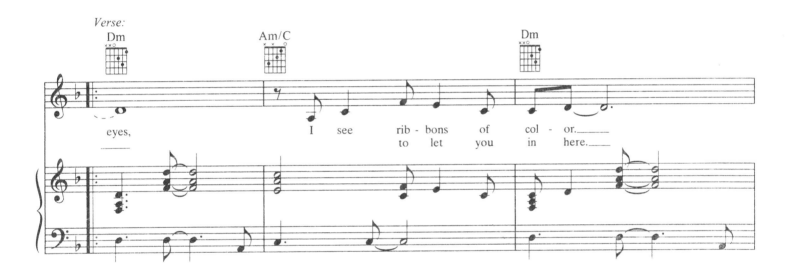

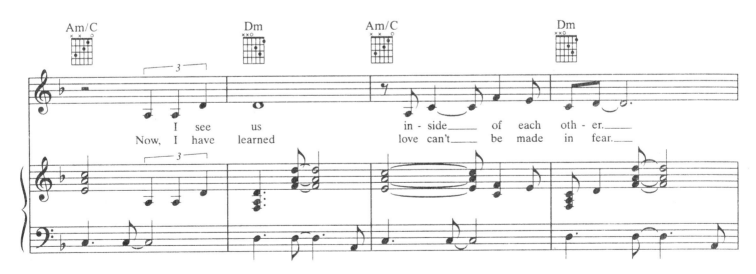

Falling into You - 5 - 1

FROM A DISTANCE

Lyrics and Music by
JULIE GOLD

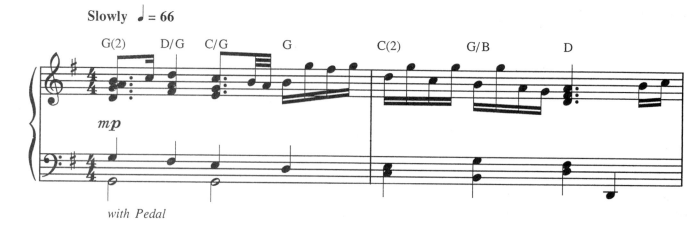

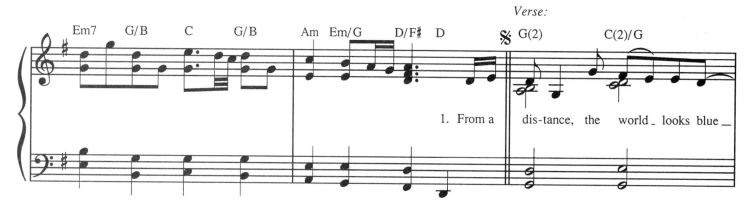

From a Distance - 4 - 1

Verse 2:
From a distance, we all have enough,
And no one is in need.
There are no guns, no bombs, no diseases,
No hungry mouths to feed.
From a distance, we are instruments
Marching in a common band;
Playing songs of hope, playing songs of peace,
They're the songs of every man.
(To Bridge:)

Verse 3:
From a distance, you look like my friend
Even though we are at war.
From a distance I just cannot comprehend
What all this fighting is for.
From a distance there is harmony
And it echos through the land.
It's the hope of hopes, it's the love of loves.

FROM THIS MOMENT ON

Words and Music by
SHANIA TWAIN and R.J. LANGE

From This Moment On - 7 - 1

32

love you,_____ I prom - ise you this._____ There is noth - ing I would-n't give,_

from this mo - ment. I will love___ you, I will love_____ you___ as

long as I live,_____ from this mo - ment

{ on.
{ on._____ }   Mm,_____ mm._____

rit.

FROZEN

Words and Music by
MADONNA CICCONE and
PATRICK LEONARD

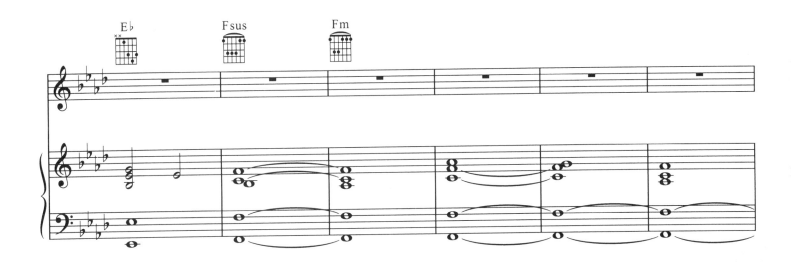

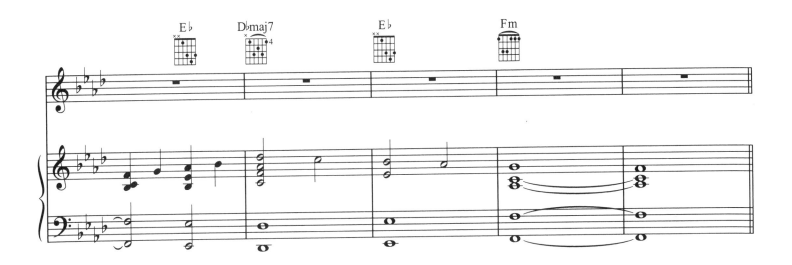

Frozen - 5 - 1

HEAVEN'S WHAT I FEEL

Words and Music by
KIKE SANTANDER

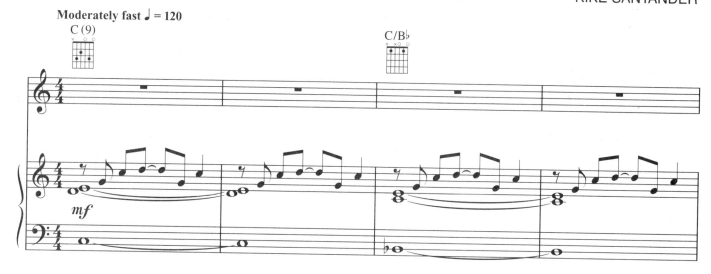

%. *Chorus:*

HIGHER GROUND

Words by
GEORGE M. GREEN

Music by
STEVE DORFF

Higher Ground - 5 - 1

48

Higher Ground - 5 - 3

50

Higher Ground - 5 - 5

From the Original Soundtrack Album "THE PREACHER'S WIFE"

I BELIEVE IN YOU AND ME

Words and Music by
SANDY LINZER and DAVID WOLFERT

1. I be-lieve in you___ and me, I be-lieve that
2. See additional lyrics

we will be in love e-ter-nal-ly.___ Well, as far as I__ can see,

52

I Believe in You and Me - 4 - 2

Verse 2:
I will never leave your side,
I will never hurt your pride.
When all the chips are down,
I will always be around,
Just to be right where you are, my love.
Oh, I love you, boy.
I will never leave you out,
I will always let you in
To places no one has ever been.
Deep inside, can't you see?
I believe in you and me.
(To Bridge:)

From the Motion Picture "THE BODYGUARD"

I WILL ALWAYS LOVE YOU

Words and Music by
DOLLY PARTON

I Will Always Love You - 5 - 1

Verse 3: Instrumental solo

Verse 4:
I hope life treats you kind
And I hope you have all you've dreamed of.
And I wish to you, joy and happiness.
But above all this, I wish you love.
(To Chorus:)

From the Motion Picture "THE MIRROR HAS TWO FACES"

I FINALLY FOUND SOMEONE

Words and Music by
BARBRA STREISAND, MARVIN HAMLISCH,
R.J. LANGE and BRYAN ADAMS

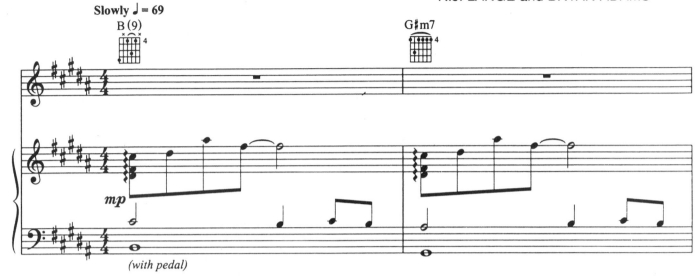

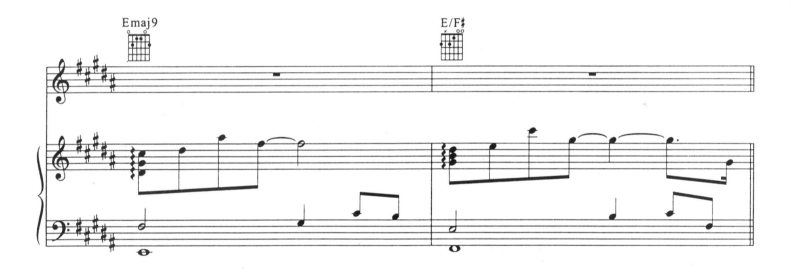

I Finally Found Someone - 8 - 1

63

66

I Finally Found Someone - 8 - 7

IF YOU ASKED ME TO

Words and Music by
DIANE WARREN

If You Asked Me To - 4 - 1

Verse 2:

71

If You Asked Me To - 4 - 4

MISSING YOU

Words and Music by
CHAS SANDFORD, MARK LEONARD
and JOHN WAITE

Missing You - 7 - 1

Missing You - 7 - 2

MY ONE TRUE FRIEND
(from "ONE TRUE THING")

Words and Music by
CAROLE BAYER SAGER, CAROLE KING
and DAVID FOSTER

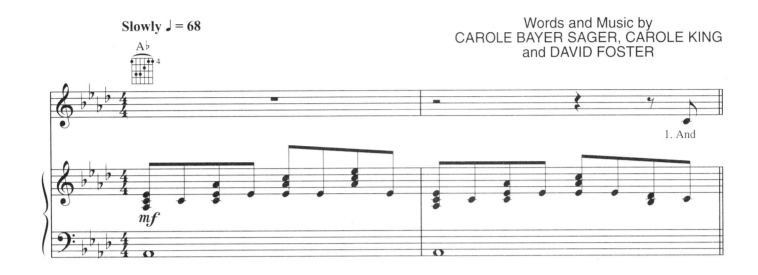

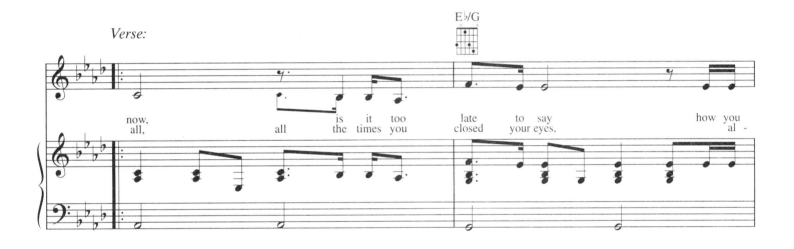

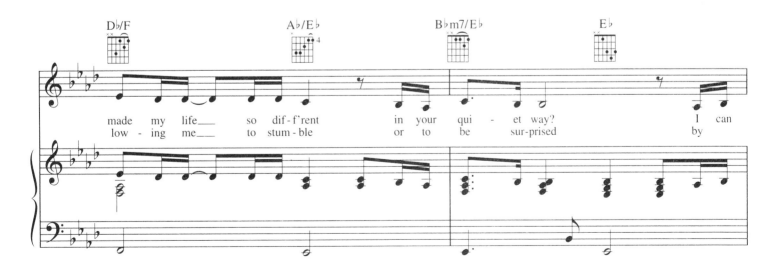

My One True Friend - 5 - 1

THE POWER OF GOOD-BYE

Words and Music by
MADONNA CICCONE
and RICK NOWELS

The Power of Good-Bye - 7 - 1

86

The Power of Good-Bye - 7 - 6

90

no more heart to bruise. There's no great-er pow-er__ than the

pow-er__ of__ good-bye.__

Verse 3:
Your heart is not open, so I must go.
The spell has been broken, I loved you so.
You were my lesson I had to learn,
I was your fortress.

Chorus 2:
There's nothing left to lose.
There's no more heart to bruise.
There's no greater power than the power of good-bye.

The Power of Good-Bye - 7 - 7

Printed in USA © 1998 Maverick/Warner Bros. Records

THE WIND BENEATH MY WINGS

Words and Music by
LARRY HENLEY and JEFF SILBAR

glo - ry,
no - ticed,

while you ___ were the
but I've ___ got it

one with all ___ the strength.
all here in ___ my heart.

A beau-ti-ful face with-out ___ a name ___
I want you to know I know ___ the truth, ___

of

for so long, ___
course I know ___ it,

a beau-ti-ful smile to hide ___ the
I ___ would be noth - ing with - out

94

The Wind Beneath My Wings - 7 - 4

96

RAY OF LIGHT

Words and Music by
MADONNA CICCONE, WILLIAM ORBIT,
CHRISTINE LEACH, CLIVE MULDOON and DAVE CURTIS

Ray of Light - 6 - 2

From the Twentieth Century-Fox Motion Picture "THE ROSE"

THE ROSE

Words and Music by
AMANDA McBROOM

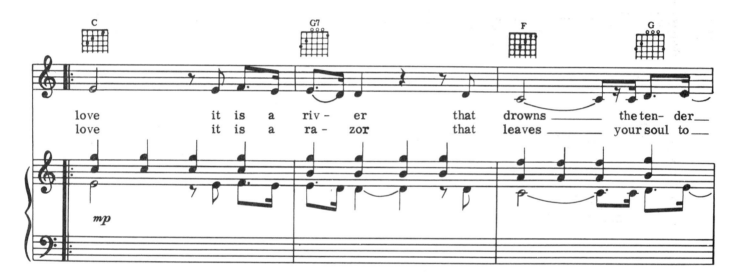

The Rose - 4 - 1

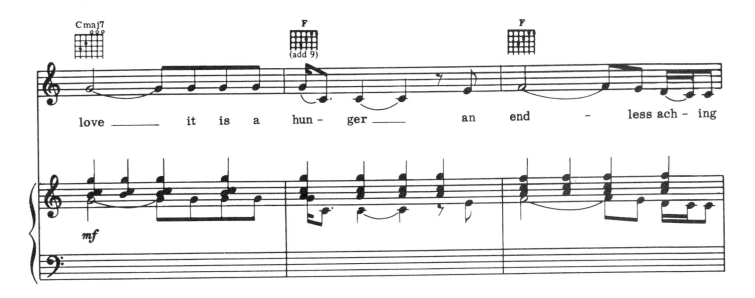

The Rose - 4 - 2

soul   a - fraid of   dy - in'   that   nev - er ____   learns to
seed   that with the   sun's ___ love   in the

live. _____   When the ___

spring   be - comes   the   rose.

play 3 times   *rit.........*

TELL HIM

Words and Music by
LINDA THOMPSON, DAVID FOSTER
and WALTER AFANASIEFF

Tell Him - 6 - 1

112

Barbra: Feed the fire with all the pas-sion you can show.__ Celine: To - night,__

love will__ as - sume__ it's place.__ Barbra: This mem-'ry time__ can - not e - rase.__

Both: Your faith will lead love where it has to__ go.__ rall.

a tempo __ Tell__ him, tell him__ that the sun and moon rise in his eyes. Reach

Verse 2:
(Barbra:)
Touch him with the gentleness you feel inside. *(C: I feel it.)*
Your love can't be denied.
The truth will set you free.
You'll have what's meant to be.
All in time, you'll see.
(Celine:)
I love him, *(B: Then show him.)*
Of that much I can be sure. *(B: Hold him close to you.)*
I don't think I could endure
If I let him walk away
When I have so much to say.
(To Chorus:)

YOU'LL SEE

Words and Music by
MADONNA CICCONE and
DAVID FOSTER

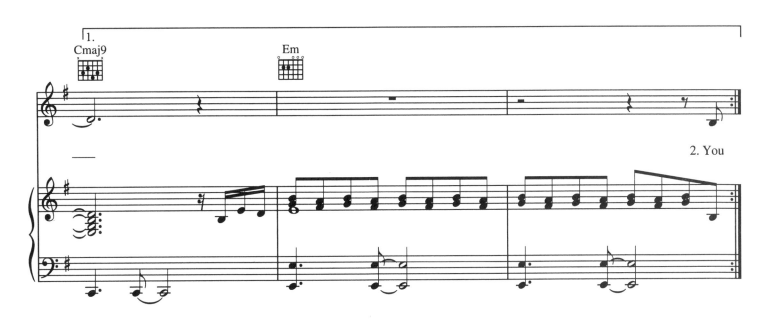

YOU'RE STILL THE ONE

Words and Music by
SHANIA TWAIN and R.J. LANGE

120

Verse 2:
Ain't nothin' better,
We beat the odds together.
I'm glad we didn't listen.
Look at what we would be missin'.
(To Bridge:)

You're Still the One - 3 - 3